Your Starring Role

(Everything you need to know about monumental nonprofit success – is found in the movies)

By Judi Ver Hoef

Copyright © 2012 by Judi Ver Hoef

Your Starring Role
by Judi Ver Hoef

Printed in the United States of America

ISBN 9781619969087

All rights reserved solely by the author. The author guarantees all contents are original and do not infringe upon the legal rights of any other person or work. No part of this book may be reproduced in any form without the permission of the author. The views expressed in this book are not necessarily those of the publisher.

www.xulonpress.com

Introduction

Your **Starring Role** provides 8 key success winning principles for those serving in a nonprofit leadership role and those responsible for hiring exceptional leaders. Nonprofit leaders are in *A League of Their Own.* Most have the compassion of *Forest Gump* but also need his determination to overcome obstacles along their way to success.

Certain lines we hear from the movies stick with us. A great movie line is not unlike a great song lyric – when the message is clear and performed in such a way to have long lasting effect. **Your Starring Role** captures the wisdom from 8 movie industry quotes and if applied will help you lead your organization to monumental success.

You have the leading role but also serve as director and executive producer. By implementing these 8 key practices consistently you're sure to receive rave revues for leading your nonprofit to greatness.

Chapter One

No Director Can Accomplish Greatness Without Vision

"Boy I got a vision and the rest of the world wears bifocals"
  – Butch Cassidy and the Sundance Kid

What's in a vision?

Vision comes from your inner voice, the voice that becomes discontented with the status quo and begins to realize there is more and better to be had. Not too long ago the Jabez Prayer came into popularity through a book which focused on its key components. One thing that Jabez prayed for was enlarging his territory. The very fact that he prayed for this shows that he could see something beyond the current state. He believed his restrictive boundaries could be expanded. Otherwise, he could visualize an exciting end result brought about by growing his territory.

Anna Mc Cowan and Jan Sykes created the following description to assist in the process of developing a vision statement. ***"A vision statement is vivid and has an idealized description of a desired outcome that inspires, energizes and helps you create a mental picture of your target. It could be a vision of a part of life, or the outcome of the project or goal. Vision statements are often confused with mission statements, but they serve a complimentary purpose capturing the essence of your vision using a simple memorable phrase that can greatly enhance the effectiveness of your vision statement."***

It's always helpful to look at a few clearly written examples before you begin. Here are some from respected and successful nonprofits and corporations:

- AVON: To be the company that best understands and satisfies the product, service and self-fulfillment needs of women—globally
- DU PONT: To be the world's most dynamic service company, creating sustainable solutions essential to a better safer and healthier life for people everywhere.
- ALZHEIMER'S ASSOCIATION: Our vision is a world without Alzheimer's
- AMERICAN HOSPITAL ASSOCIATION: A society of healthy communities, where

> all individuals reach their highest potential for health

A vision well executed has <u>purpose, provision</u> and <u>planning</u> with a strategically designed <u>process</u>. In order to come to pass it's important then for a clearly defined vision to be articulated enthusiastically and frequently. Making sure that everyone is on the same page is a challenge that leaders continually face. Perhaps more accurately stated there is a need for everyone to be in the same boat, rowing in the same direction and headed toward a unified destination. Of course it only stands to reason that implementing an on-going communication process that works is critical in making it happen. In order to articulate in an understandable manner to everyone concerned, it's necessary that your vision is fully developed accompanied by your belief that with hard work beyond familiar boundaries it is do-able. Your organization's full potential will never be reached if the leadership force of that organization is not able to visualize its greater potential.

Some people can easily be defined as visionaries but everyone has the ability to "catch hold" of a vision. However, they may digest it differently. Some begin with visualizing the end result while others begin with the steps that lead you to the end result. That's why a great communication process is just as important as having a clearly defined vision. Make your presentation brief using visual or audio aids or other "hooks" to help paint the picture. Get buy-in first from a few influencers. Then begin speaking to the broader group. I've used everything from flip charts and Power Point to props and special music to help gain and hold attention. The masses will not follow simply because there is a great vision. Great leaders have the ability to learn quickly and give away what they have learned in a way that inspires others to get on board.

Don't have a vision? Is your volunteer leadership force unable to foresee the organization's full potential? Do they not know what their role is in making it happen? Here's a success proven idea that worked for me. As chief executive, I moved from a successful chapter linked to a national volunteer health organization to a chapter of the same organization in a larger city of another state. One would think the chapter would also be larger but it was struggling. Tulsa is a city known for its philanthropy and yet this chapter's livelihood did not reflect the wonderfully generous reputation of the community.

Interestingly enough, I found a few very talented and successful business leaders on the board of directors, but they were operating without any clear vision and lacked leadership from the chief executive. These were business leaders who understood the principles of success in their corporate world but because the chapter had no defined vision; were unable to use their talents appropriately. To their detriment there was also a poor connection between the chapter and national headquarters. Unfortunately there was little vision going forward at the local level and no substantial link to the vision of our national organization as a whole.

This was a challenge that no flip chart, Power Point or prop was going to overcome in a timely manner. Since time was of the essence, I arranged for three key board members to accompany me to one of the most successful chapters in our volunteer health organization. Each board member met with a volunteer leader in their same assigned volunteer leadership role, such as fundraising, public relations and program development. We attended their board meeting and spent time with the chief executive and her key staff members. At the end of one day, our three board members actually could visualize what a great chapter looked like and had a better understanding of the steps to get there.

They returned with excitement about what we could become. For instance, the volunteer chair of our Public Relations committee came back and developed a written plan which was presented to the board and an awareness campaign was put quickly into process. The other two board members were equally excited and helped frame our new concept for growth and painted a visual picture for the full board.

Our small staff also began to understand that just as Jabez had prayed, we too could indeed see our territory increased. Remember that a good vision begins with purpose. Enlarging our territory meant that we would have the ability to provide services to more people who desperately needed our help. During the annual board's strategic planning session, we identified what provisions were needed and then proceeded to develop measurable goals and tactics which provided a pathway to follow. We all learned the importance of making sure that everyone clearly understood our vision and had taken ownership in it. The thing is – after a few years our chapter's success exceeded that of the model we once shadowed for a day. We began as a struggling organization but with a vision before us were able to grow our revenue by an average of 33% annually. We increased the number of persons served by 100% and of course when we had reached the fullness of our vision it was a time to expand the dream to meet a growing need. We became a mentoring chapter to others needing guidance.

Keep your audience plugged into the plot

Looking at things realistically not everyone wants the organization to grow. There are always

Your Starring Role

a few isolationists who fear growth and expansion. Even though they have the ability to catch hold of a vision they may chose not to. These people will not embrace even the most clearly defined futuristic vision. They are not readily moved from their comfort zone. Often they were part of the original vision which has now outgrown its relevance. Their reluctance comes from basically two fears; first there is a fear of the unknown or unfamiliar and second comes the fear of losing control. When most have grasped hold of the vision and begin to operate in their particular role of making it happen, isolationists will either reluctantly get on board or leave over time. However, some may not go without a fight, especially if they were part of the early days of foundation. I know it's a trite statement but it carries a lot of truth; "if you're not growing you're dying." That holds true for organizations as well. You are the team leader keep them motivated.

Talk to them – tell them how the process is going – communicate
Excite them with the probability of making this thing happen
Ask for feedback letting them know their opinion has merit
Make them feel appreciated

Sincerity is important – they can spot a phony

Pay attention—see around the corner before the challenge comes and prepare them
Isolate the negative
Recognize successes along the way
Ice and comfort their wounds from setbacks but keep moving them forward
Throw a big celebration when your team succeeds

Once thriving organization becomes a progressively silent motion picture

The U.S. Junior Chamber of Commerce was organized in St. Louis Missouri in 1920 with twenty-nine cities represented. By June a total of forty cities were represented and Henry Giessenbier was elected president for a full term. By 1952 there were 144,400 individual members and anyone desiring to run for political office found it helpful to have this membership on their bio. Presidents Nixon, Kennedy and Ford proudly displayed their membership in the organization which became known as the "Jaycees". Programs which found success locally were gradually taken into the overall national promotional set up. Giessenbier desired to bring about improvement through action. This was founded as a young men's leadership organization but later opened its doors to women as well. The Jaycee Creed is as follows:

"We Believe"

- That Faith in God gives meaning and purpose to human life
- That the brotherhood of man transcends the sovereignty of nations
- That economic justice can best be won by free men through free enterprise
- That government should be of laws rather than of men
- That earths great treasure lies in human personality—and
- That service to humanity is the best work of life

In 1975 my husband served as president of the organization for the state of Iowa. There were over 17,000 members just for that state alone. In 2011 the U.S. Jaycees has dwindled down to a national total of only 20,000 members. They sold and moved out of their beautiful national headquarters in Tulsa. What happened depends on who you ask. There within lies the problem. A unified vision was somehow lost along with a total misreading of community need as times continued to change. Local chapters were still doing their local thing while the national level was changing course and a unified vision never came together. No longer is there great leadership proving guidance for a clearly defined vision going forward.

Still on the Scene

The March of Dimes has a totally different story. They were instrumental in helping wipe out polio and helped families stricken along the way to prevention. When the day came that a vaccine was available and polio declined they took on another rising need to help overcome birth defects. They are still a relevant organization today.

It's important to keep the message of your vision flowing much like a promotional campaign. It's way too easy to lose momentum and direction if the main focus is not steadily kept before all to see. There are numerous distractions that come along with the potential to get a movement off track. These distractions can even come disguised as opportunities. However, they may be opportunities that do not lead to your desired destination.

I remember entering the offices of ***Senior Star***, a company owned by twin brothers Bob and Bill Thomas who have retirement communities in multiple states. I was greeted with a large tastefully created and displayed design which boldly stated the mission and vision for their company. These designs were displayed in multiple locations throughout their offices so that no employee forgets the importance of their main focus. Furthermore, anyone entering immediately knows what the company stands for and where they are headed. In addition, every new employee receives what they call a "vision card" that is pocket-sized, tri-folded and laminated. The vision card states their mission, their values and conveys the company's culture. This is a well-run company that understands the importance of purpose, provision, planning and process.

A well-written script—priceless

Your mission statement defines why you exist, your core values explain what you believe in and very important, your vision clearly states what you want to become. With these factors in place, strategies can more easily be developed. Your vision and mission statements are a complimentary pair. Following are two examples of a well written mission statement:

- AFLAC: To combine aggressive strategic marketing with quality products and services at competitive prices to provide best insurance value for consumers.
- WALT DISNEY: To make people happy

I am sure there are very few people who could see the AFLAC duck and not know what company he represents and what kind of product he promotes. A one sentence mission statement is usually attached to some clarifying values. So it is with Walt Disney. After their short but sweet mission statement you will find several defining bullet points:

- No cynicism
- Nurturing and promulgation of wholesome values
- Creating dreams, imagination
- Fanatical attention to consistency and detail
- Preservation and control of Disney magic

Good managerial and organizational skills are needed to bring your vision to fruition. A great leader knows that if their vision does not center on real need then moving forward is futile. A successful vision will hit both the hearts and minds of your targeted constituents.

I Have a Dream!

It goes without saying that the most well-known vision ever articulated came from the historic speech by Martin Luther King, "I Have a Dream." King didn't need flip charts or other visual aids because he was one of America's most dynamic speakers. It was easy to get caught up in the emotions of his words but you can also learn valuable knowledge about how to structure your message. He began by invoking the past legacy of Abraham Lincoln and the Emancipation Proclamation which had been signed about 100 years earlier. He then went on to describe problems which continued to plague America's people of color despite the hope proclaimed through the Proclamation. Thirdly, he enumerated the pressing civil rights issues of the day and by the fourth point he was able to bring forward "his dream" by providing a glimpse of a better future for all and a better understanding of what we could become.

Few visions will carry this kind of historical weight but the structure of King's speech provides a helpful guide for preparing to communicate your vision to a wider circle. It's important to start by reviewing your organizations beginning foundational purpose, followed by the current status. The next step is critical. Identify problems, concerns and the need for change. These preliminary points provide a platform for you to paint a picture of your organization's future impact. Otherwise, focus on the why, why now, what and how.

As stated before, it's important to keep your message flowing. Make sure that both staff and board members can articulate the vision by giving them simple bullet points and tools. Create a common set of key messages that can be integrated into all communications. Whether hard or soft copy, every important communication piece should carry aspects of the vision. This can also be included on business cards. Don't confuse strategies with vision. Your vision is what you want to become not how you're going to get there although strategies are of the utmost importance. A great vision will help people think and act in a way that takes them in a new direction enthusiastically. Bring spark to every mundane meeting by incorporating your organization's vision in an exciting manner.

Although many groups need to understand your vision, different groups have varied communication needs and not everybody needs or wants to move along the process at the same speed. For instance, how will stakeholders be impacted by the change of direction toward a newly defined vision? What information do they need to move along in the process and at what point will they need it? These are questions that require answers because each organization has its own uniqueness and characteristics of their stakeholders.

A happy ending

How will you know if you're process is successful? You will begin to see a shared acceptance evolve and an understanding of the rationale for the vision and if relevant—the change. A shared desire for your organization's future is easily discerned by your team as their effort begins to help navigate through change. In addition, you will see teamwork that is consistent with the vision and decisions that break away from past inconsistencies will become the norm.

Your Starring Role

This is an important role for leaders to play. It's no time to drop the reigns just because you're off to a good start. Continuing check-ups are imperative. Control your excitement to just "git er done" while resting on your assumption that all is well. This move or lack thereof can end up causing the movement to lose precious time and resources as no roadblock will remain hidden forever. If you don't have all the facts – don't assume that all is well. Stay engaged and informed so that your decisions will not be made from one who like an ostrich has his head in the sand. Don't be the one who lets ego enter in from yourself or your leadership team. Create an environment that rewards information gathering and a comfortable atmosphere to be truthful when a course change is needed. The vision does not change but the map in getting there may have to be changed along the way. In fact you can be prepared for this.

Plan for short term wins along the way and this will help bolster a long term commitment. Short term wins will provide momentum to show that "its" working and will help continue to shape exit of the "old" while solidifying confidence in the "new" as developed strategies move the process along.

Chapter Two

The Right Casting – The Right Place – The Right Time

"The way to prevent war is be ready for it"
—Cleopatra

Guide to build a winning cast

We often hear leaders say "people are our greatest asset. That's only partly right. Having the right people in the right place at the right time is most important. A great leader does have some identifiable qualities.

General Norman Schwarzkopf Jr. certainly qualified in the category of greatness. He only had two simple rules: ***1.When placed in command take charge 2. Do what is right.***

Other stars playing successful roles

In order to get the "feel" for various leadership characteristics let's look at some additional examples of exceptional greatness. **Rev. Billy Graham** has been a spiritual mentor to the nation and to every president for decades. At the time of this writing he is ninety-three and just completed his final book called "Nearing Home." Even in his final phase of life he is demonstrating a leadership quality - this time with instruction on how to face aging issues, both spiritual and secular. Reverend Graham has easily recognizable characteristics. He is a man of integrity with morale values. He accepts his role in life – knowing who he is, why he is here and where he is going. He's been able to separate the important from the unimportant and counsel others to do the same. His vision has always been greater than himself.

One of the nation's favorite presidents, **Ronald Reagan** was likeable and he understood the importance of this in carrying forth his message. Wrapped up in his likability was a kind, humble and decent individual often using humor rather than viciousness to make a point. He was able to offer "hope" backed up by the actions to achieve it. Some called him the eternal optimist. He saw us as the "City on a Shining Hill."

His description of America went something like this; hopeful, big hearted, idealistic, caring, decent and fair. As a great leader, he understood the importance of delegating and the pitfalls of micro-managing. To his credit he was able to admit to his mistakes and change course for rectification. Last but certainly not least, he worked at having a balanced life spending time out of the White House as he said to "keep perspective."

Winston Churchill is another leader whose qualities are interesting. He was a man with steely determination during WII. When looking at some of his historical video footage, I am moved by his amazing public speaking ability. Just through his words and inflection, he was able to lift people up during a very difficult time in history. He had an innate ability to earn people's trust quickly, partly because they saw him as such a man of courage. He had the ability to help others reach their level of greatness which is certainly a sign of a great leader.

President **George Washington** was a do what you say – say what you mean guy. He made all decisions based on principle and had a keen observation which carried him through the process. He was described as a well-balanced individual with a strong ability to foster relationships. He was able to learn from defeat and use what he learned to bring about victory. He's noted as saying, "Be humble you are not greater than the cause you represent."

John F. Kennedy's presidency was short lived but he led with a compelling vision for America.

Even his biggest critics admired his leadership qualities as he spelled out the New Frontier image and later on the Moon Project. He learned about peaceful cooperation after the consequences of the Cuban Missile Crisis. His collegial decision making model was a consensus seeking tool which ensured that problems were debated. He selected advisors that reflected the strengths and weaknesses of his policy experience.

Prime Minister **Margaret Thatcher** has been touted as the right person in the right place at the right time. She herself was not an original thinker but rather had a powerful collection of beliefs that served her well. The ideas were not new but were put into operation by her remarkable ability to lead. When she became leader, Britain was on the brink of disaster. She is the only woman to ever lead in Britain's history; a scenario that America has yet to see. She had the courage to see opportunity and take it. She was decisive in a time of crisis and she had clear beliefs supported by physical stamina and a great intellectual capacity. The people believed in her and re-elected her three times bringing her years of service to eleven.

Finding a star in your talent search

This snapshot of a few of the world's great leaders provides some helpful fodder when you begin your search and hire process for a leadership position. Following is a list of competencies to look for to identify great leadership abilities or in developing your own:

- Can foresee the consequences of decisions
- Hire's the right subordinates and creates winners
- Projects the vision clearly and with enthusiasm
- Is skilled at gaining support
- Continually produces more than expected
- Sets standards higher than other like-organizations
- Solves problems effectively without negative side effects
- Writes and speaks to achieve maximum impact
- Respects and is respected
- Is confident and believes in self
- Others seek his guidance
- Knows what's important and what's not important
- Is led by respected values and principles
- Leads with purpose
- Knows his casts individual leadership needs and provides
- Has a good balance between detailed focus and creativity
- Honesty and integrity are evident

- Past history reflects great successes
- Is not content with average or status quo
- Will not quit when the going gets rough
- Has the ability to see further and deeper than his followers
- Will not sell out the organization or his team for personal gain
- Knows how to develop and lead through an effective process

Perception becomes reality in and out of the movies

Before I became CEO of a volunteer health organization, I served on the management team of a local hospital. One of my responsibilities was processing hospital complaints and in turn to look for any negative trends that might develop. I began to see more and more complaints about the head physician of our emergency room. Most had to do with his bedside manner. It was clear to all hospital personnel that his technical abilities were way above par. In fact, I always said if anyone in my family ever needed an emergency room doctor he would be my choice.

I understood that he didn't have the best bedside manner and his way of communicating was somewhat short and direct but in spite of that he and I had a pretty good rapport—so, I went to him and said, "Doc we're seeing a considerable spike in complaints about your bedside manner." "Enough so that I felt it important to let you know." His response was not exactly unexpected, he said, "I'm in the business of saving lives not making nice." In the technical sense, he was right but we were talking about patient perception which is their only point of reference. A healthcare provider needs consumers to survive just like any other service or product provider.

I had been instructed when complaints reached a certain plateau to make the Administrator aware. I did just that and within a few weeks a member of the hospital board of trustees asked for my file and the administrator shortly thereafter terminated the doctor. A new emergency room doctor was hired who had a great personality. He treated every patient with compassion and had a warm smile that put you immediately at ease. However, it was evident to those of us who knew anything about a physician's technical ability that his was about average. However, from then on we got great feedback from our patients on their emergency room service. This example clearly reveals that there is something very important beyond technical ability.

It's not enough just to hire someone with stellar educational qualifications – it's equally important to find an individual with high emotional intelligence and characteristics that will fit your team. Cary Cherniss and Daniel Goleman explain this is their publication, *The Emotionally Intelligent Workplace*. During twenty-five years their research has pointed out the importance of emotional intelligence which includes self-confidence, initiative, and teamwork as making a significant difference in performance. Their book is a recommended read for those who are interested in how to select for, measure and improve emotional intelligence in individuals, groups and organizations.

Character counts

Very early on in my working career I was hired to assist the Public Relations Director for a health services provider. We had been friendly acquaintances before my hire. It became apparent that she ran a lose ship and because the Administrator was far from being a micro manager she felt that she had pretty free reign.

Because I had responsibilities in addition to those in public relations, I too had somewhat regular contact with the Administrator. As time went on she became more involved in personal activities on company time.

At first she would tell me she was going to meet clients. However, as time went on she didn't hide the fact that she was involved in personal activities. She did expect me to cover for her. I noticed that the Administrator was calling our office more frequently to speak with her. At first he seemed fine with my answer, "She's out of the office right now can I take a message?" Then he started asking where she was and if I knew with what client she was to meet. I told him if I knew and if I didn't know I merely said, I'm not sure but may I take a message? One day he called me into his office to let me know that she had been fired. She contacted me to tell me that she was terribly upset that I did not cover for her and actually to this day she may still think the blame was on me for the firing. A person who gets fired for not performing the job for which they were hired can only look in the mirror. She was creative and had genuine interpersonal skills to offer but was lacking in integrity and the leadership ability expected of her.

Typecasting for greatness

If given the opportunity it's best to find the right person in the beginning rather than to try and reshape them afterward. Behavior is most difficult to change. I developed a grading system for positions at each level of our nonprofit organization. Each employee was given a grade in line with the system. Grades were given for both technical and emotional intelligence culminating in a grade for overall performance. The goal of course is to get everyone to their highest possible grade ranging from four (4) which is lowest; to one (1) which is highest. If you want your organization to soar with the eagles work toward the goal of no grades below a two (2) and not more than fifty percent (50%) should be at that level. The rest should be solid ones. Here's a hint, if the leader of the organization does not rate at a level one (1) don't expect for the rest as a whole to either. Having the right leader(s) in place is critical to rise to monumental success.

By using a grading system throughout your interview and hiring process you will most likely improve your listening skills, ask more probing questions and retain important information for the feedback review with your search team.

Opening lines critical to success

A way to prevent a battle later on is to put an exacting effort in on the front end before you're faced with a crisis. A crisis can easily happen by having the wrong person in place doing the wrong thing at the wrong time. I've done it both ways and can attest to the importance of using a grading system.

I've been guilty in the past of hiring on credentials alone. But, on a positive note, I was able to learn from this mistake. We had an opening for a leader in a region plagued by a strong competitor. We interviewed a young man with a doctorate degree although with limited experience in the field. I thought it might be a good idea to out-credential our competitor. Not unlike the emergency room fiasco we had a person with some terrific book learning but very little insight on how to "lead" and how to communicate with competition. I didn't have to let him go, he figured it out for himself and exited.

Having made some hiring mistakes along the way, I was determined to get it right. I gathered information from several successful HR professionals and reviewed at least a dozen books on the subject. I also visited with several very successful HR directors to gain insight. Our leadership team then took bits and pieces of wisdom from each in order to develop a system that best fit our organization's current size and need. Finding the right "hire" or teammate is a little like finding your soul mate. You don't need, or want for that matter, someone who agrees with you 100% of the time. Nor do you necessarily want someone who exactly mirrors your strengths and weaknesses. Knowing the leadership strengths of your existing team members will help define what you're looking for to fill the vacant position. So, before you even get into the hiring process there is work to be done internally.

We started by using a book called *Strengths Based Leadership* by Tom Rath and Barry Conchie. Every employee was given a copy and asked to take the StrengthsFinder 2.0 test in order to identify their leading strengths. We were able then to develop a chart that provided an overview of our team strengths revealing any gaps we might have. Knowing the strengths of one another also helped each of us to navigate better as an individual team member.

This information is equally valuable to find the "right" person for a particular position. Our team developed a description of qualities the "right" person would need to possess. These included the usual academic and technical aspects and as mentioned before, characteristics associated with emotional intelligence. Simply by reviewing our existing team strengths' chart we could identify exactly which strengths were needed to hire right for the vacancy. In the book *Strengths Based Leadership* they divide four domains of leadership into the following: ***executing, influencing, relationship building and strategic thinking.*** It stands to reason that you don't need an entire department made up of strategic thinkers. A good balance of strengths is optimal. There are many good resources out there that can help in identifying strengths. This was the one that worked well for us.

What's next? After you develop your exact "needs" you will have identified information needed to write a perfectly targeted search ad and to create a great set of targeted interview questions.

Next it is important to develop a quick check list for the person scanning your incoming applications. This list should have the priority qualifications needed for your vacant position. After individuals are selected as possible candidates for the interview process, a brief phone conversation will help narrow the field even further. An initial phone visit can help you evaluate how well he fits your need and if he's appropriate for a team interview. Resumes that arrive without a cover letter are immediate discards as well as those with misspellings or grammatical errors. This includes those that arrive via email which is most prevalent in todays' culture. This is the candidates' calling card and should be presented in perfection to show that they have given proper attention and care. The impression you get from this first contact will provide evidence of what you can expect from him if he becomes your employee.

Once you have selected candidates for the interview process, I recommend sending them a questionnaire to fill out and return via email. The questions can be worded in such a way to hit upon at least some of the more important emotional intelligence and leadership strengths desired for the position. Here are some things to watch for - does the candidate get the form completed and returned in a timely manner? How do the answers stack up in regard to the skills needed that you previously identified?

Provide each member of the interview team with a copy of the original resume and application form along with results from the email questionnaire and any other relative materials. This provides a quick snapshot of the candidate before entering into the interview process. It's important to create a comfortable atmosphere for the interview. Make sure the room temperature is dialed for comfort and welcome your candidate in a friendly manner offering some small talk as they get settled. Allow for self-introductions from the interview team which should include no more than four (4) to six (6) people depending on the level of the vacant position. Make sure you explain the process upfront and include whatever information you chose to provide about your organization and the position. How you conduct the opening introductions and pleasantries can be helpful in getting the most and best from your candidate. The more comfortable he becomes the better the potential for a real and honest interview. Provide an opportunity both at the beginning and the end for the candidate to have freedom to speak or ask questions.

Developing a list of questions that gets to a candidates' educational background and technical ability is pretty self-explanatory. Therefore, the following list of potential interview questions is mostly meant to provide an example for interviewers to get a deeper look at emotional intelligence and leadership strengths. Have the interview team meet before-hand taking a section of questions from the completed prepared list. Every candidate must be asked the same general questions other than ones related to their resume and follow-ups to their answers.

- Can you tell us about a significant failure and success that you have experienced and what you learned from them?
- Can you recall a time there was a crisis in your workplace? What was it, how did you respond and what was the outcome?
- If you could only name one thing, what one thing would you say makes you most frustrated?
- What is the one trait in others that you find most difficult to tolerate?
- When you think about your future – what do you see?
- What would you most like to change about yourself and what have you done to start the process?
- What do you like to do for fun?
- What's your best process for learning something new?
- Which of the following best describes you; one who prefers to deal with short term concrete tangible issues or one who

prefers more abstract or conceptual long-term issues and why?
- Can you recall a time when your self-assurance seemed to increase your ability to do something extremely challenging?
- Tell about a time you identified a problem and developed a solution that worked
- Can you tell us about a time that you served on a team that was not functioning well? What did you do? Did it help?
- What is the title of the last book you read?
- What qualities do you seek most in a friend?
- What thought process did you go through before considering to apply for this position?
- Can you describe a time when your loyalty to your workplace stood out for all to see?
- Is there a time when you have been in the process of bringing about change? If so what was your role and what was the outcome?
- What three words would best describe your workplace strengths?
- I think we have all been involved in conflict at one time or another. Tell me a time that you were in conflict with another – why did it happen and how did you handle it? What was the outcome?
- What does the term active listening mean to you? Can you provide an example when you have used it?

- What's your sense of humor like and how has it benefited you in the workplace?
- Do your best results come when you are working independently or when you are working within a group?
- How would you describe the principles or values that are most important to the way you do your job?
- What have you done specifically in the past year to keep current on knowledge related to your field in today's competitive market?
- What tends to get you down emotionally and what do you do to get back up?
- How do you like for your expectations to be communicated to you and how will you and your manager know if they are on track for being met?
- Have you participated as a positive change agent in the workplace in recent times and if so what was the change and how did you help bring it about?
- Tell us about a time that you persuaded others to see something your way or to sell an idea

This list of questions provides an example of how they can provide broad-based answers with an opportunity for them to provide open-ended depth. I also like to throw in an unexpected humorous question to get a sense of how the candidate will respond. For instance, "If it rains to make the grass and trees grow why does it have to rain on the sidewalk? You might be surprised by the response you get. If most of his answers have been researched and rehearsed in some way or another. An injected silly question might just provide a sense of how he reacts when rhythm is interrupted and something unexpected happens.

To be continued

Although the first round team interview can bring out a lot of information, don't make a decision based on those results. During the first round interview, your team can use the scoring system you have developed from exact qualifications needed for the vacant position. Immediately following the interview process your team may share their scored results and provide rationale for their answers.

It's then time for second round interviews to be scheduled when all first round candidates have finished theirs and have been scored by the team. Don't settle. Don't ever settle just to fill your dance card. It's always better to put in the time to find the right person rather than to settle for the best you can find at the time. If a candidate shows up without doing his homework on your organization, that is grounds for dismissing him as a possibility – even if you like his other qualities.

We are in the age of technology and information therefore candidates should come well-armed for the interview.

If you don't have consensus from the interview team or belief that you have one or more great candidates, go back to the drawing board and spread a wider net. Make sure that everyone connected to your organization has a clear definition of who you're looking for to fill the position. There's also the possibility of outreach to "non-lookers" which are sometimes called passive candidates. These are potential candidates already employed somewhere else; but perhaps with the exact qualifications you need. They are well-known for their success and may just be ripe for change and advancement. Letting them know of your opportunity might just turn into a win/win.

It is possible that your organization may want to use a "head hunter". If so make sure that you still do your homework upfront so that they have all the critical criteria needed to find the right candidates.

Your second round does not need the full interview team. However, the immediate supervisor and at least one person who sat in on the first round should participate. Your list of questions for this round can be developed from gaps found through scoring of the first round. If there were answers that need more clarification this is a time to get at those. The second round is truly drill-down time. Make sure you've covered every angle. If a candidate brings his portfolio be sure everyone has a chance to review it. If relevant to the position you can ask a candidate to provide a short verbal or written presentation. This can provide volumes of information including how he works under pressure and the quality of his work.

Do your research before offering the role

Even if you believe you have found the right person don't make a final move until references are thoroughly checked. I like to have at least four. It's best to have one personal reference, one person who has been managed by the candidate, one person who has managed the candidate and one who has been his peer. I also like to use Google, Facebook and other sources just to see what I can find further about the candidate. I have often been pleasantly surprised by doing this but at least once, found information that was not pleasing.

After references are checked, a thorough criminal and financial background check by a professional is critical. It is also helpful to get a copy of any driving citations if they will be traveling on behalf of the organization. I have witnessed dangerous hires cut off at the pass through proper background checking. People who are trying to hide something will often list only the counties where they know they have no criminal records on file. It is wise to conduct your search beyond only the counties they list. ***Information Searches Incorporated*** for instance makes it a practice to search surrounding counties and if a record is found they give the client an option of adding that county to their request list. Sometimes people will change their social security number by one or they will transpose numbers to keep a search from hitting on their record. Using a similar name or a middle name is also used as a ploy to lead the searcher astray. Many national data bases are outdated therefore, it's important to know about your source beforehand. Know what sources the background check firm is using before you put your trust in them. ***ISI Inc.*** also conducts outsourced searches for several other national firms. Searchers from the firm have been surprised to learn that sometimes a major firm is not interested in a felony found beyond the counties listed in their original territory request due to the added cost. I'm a firm believer in paying an extra few dollars up front rather than paying a huge price later on in more ways than one.

To sum it all up don't try to hurry the process or skip steps. Cover all your bases before making a decision. All too often the decision made is haste is later regretted.

Building a cast that connects

Having the right person in the right place at the right time is as important as building a team that works in synergy making the most of their own talent while complimenting the talents of their team mates. A great team does not just happen it takes a concentrated effort.

Making things even more difficult some teams are scattered out over several satellite offices. Team building takes planning and specialized actions.

Integrating a new cast member

Every time there is a change within a team, there is a need to re-build. It is most critical that your management team functions in sync. When a key member leaves it's always an adjustment for the others. This is especially true if the person who left has been instrumental in bringing about a generous portion of the organization's success. Anyone appointed to fill those shoes will be met with some skepticism. Make sure the newbie has an ample orientation which includes scheduled meetings with each management team member individually so that they can learn a little more about one another. I know it sounds a bit strange but there is a similarity to some level of grief when a great team member leaves. It takes a little time to get re-oriented. Time is not what you have a lot of when there are stretch goals before you.

- Have a welcome party
- Determine who will be the best match for the new team member
- Assign this person as a "buddy" for the first few weeks
- Take the whole group to lunch a few time during the first couple of months
- Make sure she meets important stakeholders within the first few weeks
- Encourage staff from outlining offices to welcome her on board
- Give her a "quick" project destined to succeed (this will help build her self-confidence as well as confidence in her from others)
- Stay in close contact with other management team members to make sure they are adjusting to the change
- Orientation is not completed in one day (make sure it comes in phases and covers all the bases)

When you are the new leader of the team

- Realize it's not easy to get used to a new boss especially if they have worked well with the prior one and held him in high esteem

Your Starring Role

- Go on a listening tour prepared to take notes and do just that: (Ask their opinion on how things are going and find out what recommendations they might have)
- Don't talk too much about how you did it in your last organization

- During a second meeting let them know that you understand what goals lie ahead and that you have confidence that working together it can be done (This is a time to go over some of the goal details so that they know that you are on point
- Have a social get-to-gather to help create a friendly work atmosphere
- Make frequent one-on-one contact in the first few weeks so that they quickly get used to your personality and know that you are interested in them as important members of the team
- Have weekly management team meetings making sure everyone has a voice to articulate successes, concerns or ask questions (include at least one fun exercise for the meeting)
- Don't wait too long to hold a management team retreat (make sure agenda is relevant, exciting and has ample time for team building activities

- Identify one or two influencers you can trust in the first few weeks to help carry the load of moving actions along to meet goal (these should be individuals that have influence and are respected on the team
- Insure that the vision is understood by all and that goals and objectives are clearly written and applied to individual action plans
- Track and control team performance toward goals
- Put equal effort in building team chemistry as well as team performance and understand that team building is an ongoing process

If you're building a brand new team from the ground up. I recommend doing it in phases. Since much of the chief executives time is spent in the ongoing development of a strong management team it's better to start with a few depending on the size of your organization. Once you get the few operating at a level of excellence then they can be helpful in orientating the next phase of new members. If you get too many new ones at once it goes beyond herding cats and becomes a little more like trying to keep a dozen ping pong balls under water at the same time.

Chapter Three

Enjoy Today's Win but Not without a Plan for Tomorrow

"Life moves pretty fast if you don't stop and look around you could miss it."
—Ferris Buellers' Day Off

Don't forget to hand out awards for great performance

Team members have to feel connected to the cause with a sense of recognition for achievement to become truly committed. Some of this is self-generated but it's also up to you, the leader to create an environment that cultivates this kind of commitment. Life moves very quickly in the hub of a nonprofit, therefore you can easily overlook a short term win while advancing toward the ultimate goal. Remember when we talked about the "right" people in the "right" place at the "right" time doing the "right" thing? These are your greatest assets and deserve regular appreciation which in turn heightens their morale and enhances your organization's image.

It's easy to be drawn in to spending more time on underperformers in order to help them improve. It's actually more important to make sure your over-achievers are shown recognition and appreciation in ways that keep them motivated, appreciated and connected. A good rule to follow is to give 80% of your time to your great performers and 20% to those who fall short. Therefore, when celebrating a win make sure that the "right" individuals receive their "right" due reward along with a celebration for the entire team.

Although it has its place, money isn't the only way to reward performers. Over the years I had several low cost initiatives that I used. One idea that I found on line consisted of little cards of thanks and appreciation about the size of a business card that fit inside an envelope. In addition, every employee had a little mailbox just big enough to hold the card. I was surprised to see how effective those little personalized notes became. I also created individualized certificates of appreciation based on the particulars of a team member's situation. Sometimes I made the reward personalized to something I knew about them. I gave a gift certificate to the local toy store to one of our working moms who always exceeded goal. There was another who was a diehard sports fan for her alumni college team. I got her a signed team photo and thanked her for a job well done. Common sense and creativity work well in developing a good reward system. Don't always do the expected; a surprise reward is always appreciated.

It really just gets back to the basic principle to treat and recognize others just as you would like to be treated and recognized. People who feel appreciated by you, their leader, are more connected to your organization and more consistently do their best. This in turn also means they will most likely treat your organization's constituents in the same way.

Believe it or not, sometimes recognition can come in the form of more work. Over-achievers, or exceeders as I like to call them, enjoy a challenge. Perhaps there is a special project still in the hopper waiting to be launched – this is a great way to recognize a person's previous win and put them in play for the next one.

Everyone likes to be on a winning team regardless of what position they play. So, make sure the entire team shares in the glory of the win. Those who participated in the win but not at their level best may be inspired to move it up a notch during the next assignment. You will often see a team member's professional growth just by them serving on an exceptional team and sharing in the victory.

It's difficult for a visionary to stop and smell the roses because they are already planting the next flower garden in their mind. However, it is important for self-awareness and satisfaction to make a conscious effort to celebrate your wins. Celebrating a win can be equated with providing the "pot" for the gold at the end of a rainbow. Your accomplishment should have ongoing benefit but the celebration provides an opportunity to gather all the benefits of the win together for personal satisfaction. A celebration also provides a platform for your next process in winning.

Enjoy the award-winning performance but be prepared for tomorrow

Once in a while even a blind squirrel finds a nut. Occasionally you can have a win without the desired planning process but this is not optimal by any means. There has probably been more written about strategic planning than any other subject for obtaining success. However, sometimes the plan can become more complicated than the actual implementation of the project.

Your process can be as simple or as complicated as you make it. The most important thing is to develop a good plan that has solid reference to past results with do-able but challenging goals for the future. Do your homework by making sure that you obtain feedback from your constituents. The only real truth your organization has is the overall perception of those you serve, those who

Your Starring Role

support the cause and those who make up the team. This is a time when your perception doesn't count because you might be wrong. A movie goer makes up his own mind about the plot, the acting and the way the story is presented. The opinion of the movie goer will become his reality regardless of what the writers, producers and actors may have thought. So it is with an organization, those partaking of your services or those taking notice of your organization overall will ultimately shape its true reality. Perception is truth to the beholder.

Yesterday's outdated strategic planning process will not work in today's fluid world. As a leader of a nonprofit today you already know this. However, unfortunately an update in your strategic planning process may not have kept up with the times. It might be time for a "re-make" in your planning process.

However, the basic questions to be answered haven't changed. Who are you as an organization? What trends are affecting you and how are you positioned to contend in the market place with your competitors? Exactly where are you and how did you get this far? Where can you go and where do you want to go from here? What barriers may be in your way? How can you move them or get around them? What will it look like if you reach your destination?

Once all of these questions are answered conduct a private screening to make sure your key influencers believe it's on target. In the process be prepared to answer these questions. What will it cost in real dollars? Where will the dollars come from? What is the plan to make people aware of what we're doing and why? Can the need be easily explained in line with a rapidly changing environment? How will you make it happen? How will you know you have succeeded? Helpful key phrases for your new planning process include; past performance measurables, leave funding and service vulnerabilities on the cutting room floor, meet poor reviews head-on, add new ideas to the script for fundraising and programs, perform toward financial independence, re-writes are inevitable and reach "the end" with appropriate editing.

Past performance measurables:

"Just the facts mam" – Review bottom line numbers from three categories: 1) Organization 2) Programs 3) Operations. As mentioned in chapter one it is important that both vision and mission statements are current and relevant. Look at not only your own results but also that of your competitors. All the data you can gather going forward will help in creating a winning plot for your future.

Leave funding and service vulnerabilities on the cutting floor

There's some real work to be done here. It's a time to consider trends, past results, competition, economy issues and every aspect of fund development. Do the same in looking at your program area. What are you still doing just because you've always done it? What has changed? How does technology influence? What solutions have already been implemented? Where can you cut cost without cutting value?

Meet poor reviews head-on

Don't be afraid to pick up the review page. Make sure that you have a built in evaluation process and take an honest look at it. Look for weak links and wavering support. Don't be defensive and don't make excuses where downward or negative trends are evident. Create an honest assessment.

Add new ideas to the script for fundraising and programs

This is where you need to spend some time and go for the Academy Award! Make sure that your plan exceeds the average or expected and strive to exceed what your competitor has done in the past at least in some areas. Use every possible cost effective cutting-edge resource available. Plan to do the unexpected or the sure-to-get-noticed in a way that will take your organization to a whole new level. Expand your target audience and you will expand your donor prospects. Create innovative ways of doing old things in a new way to reach even better results. This is another one of those places where you have to have the right people leading the effort. People too tied to old securities will find it very uncomfortable to step out into something new. You need someone who can not only see an exciting vision for the future but also bring others along on the journey.

Diverse strengths can move the process forward. *Visionaries* can look outside of the box and see things beyond where you've been before to bring about that needed competitive edge. Your *analysts* can see any pitfalls to be addressed while your *promoters* will know how to "brand" it. The team *implementers* will get it launched and head up the effort to see it through.

Perform toward financial independence

This does not mean that as a nonprofit you won't have to rely on donors or supporters. What it does mean is that your organization should never be put in a position to be heavily influenced because of a high level of financial dependency from any one support resource. Otherwise don't sell out your cause for an almighty dollar in your planning or any other time. Go broader not deeper for a more secure pathway. Make sure that every dollar in the revenue budget is connected to a detailed action in the activity or tactic plan. For instance, if dollars needed are to come from individuals make sure that a list has been created with names and projected amounts. I recommend applying a comfort range to the amount. For instance, if the ask to Mr. Jones is going to be $20,000, what is your comfort range in the result? Here is an example: $20,000 = 70% comfort; $15,000 = 80% comfort; $10,000 = 98% comfort. If you do not have a 100% comfort range then put a lesser amount in the actual budget but keep the higher amount in your development action plan.

Re-writes are Inevitable

The economy, technology and other factors are ever-changing in our fast-paced world today so, don't write your plan in stone. Make sure it is a working document that can be adjusted as needed. Unless you have suffered a set-back of disastrous proportion, make changes to move you forward not backward. Even then look for a way out don't take defeat lying down. I was leading a nonprofit organization during the ravenous flood back in 1993. Local grant and corporate funding that had already been promised to us was rescinded and given to the urgent disaster needs. On top of that we had to cancel our largest fundraising event. We changed our plan and created a proposal to our parent organization asking for help due to unforeseeable circumstances. Because I had done my homework and given exceptional detail about the expected long term effects we were able to get a grant without a necessity to repay. In addition, I sent requests to other funding sources outside of our affected area and was able to get two more grants. We ended up right on target with budget in a year that could have been disastrous. It's just a matter of turning to excuses or alternative possibilities. Otherwise, always fail forward.

Reach the end with rave reviews

Some movie producers seem to know how to have a hit time after time. They appear to know what their ever-changing audience wants over time. So it is with nonprofit leadership you have to have your finger on the pulse of your people. There are numerous ways to collect data. A couple have been most effective in my past experience. The SAQ or self–administered questionnaire is one we are all familiar with. Make sure that every program and service you provide has a mechanism in place to gain feedback. Questionnaires should be made available at every program site or they can be sent via email and even the good ole snail mail process. Begin with brief instructions explaining how to return the completed form. Explain your purpose for gathering feedback and consider asking questions that gauge the participant's knowledge or skill level before the program. Make sure that you collect baseline data that will focus on outcomes centering on what the program intends to change in participants. You also have to have what many call the "it" factor. For such a little word it carries a ton of weight. "It" consists of having a vision of excellence, not losing sight of the vision, making sure there is a pathway for obtaining the vision, knowing how to bring others along, changing the pathway if necessary and never giving up until the vision becomes reality. You will know you have completed a successful endeavor by reporting and staying in sync with your measurables along the way.

A focus group although using fewer people can bring about more detailed response. The ability to have a conversation about details can sometimes be more helpful than brief answers on a questionnaire. Both have their place but can bring about helpful information.

Chapter Four

Don't be led by Disruptions

"I don't want to be a product of my environment; I want my environment to be a product of me"
—*The Departed*

Don't wander from the original script unless it's warranted

We don't usually think about planning for the unexpected unless it's something big like creating a disaster plan which certainly has become more prevalent in today's environment. However, the day to day unexpected disruptions can keep you spinning if you don't have a pre-planned process in place to deal with them. This again, illuminates the importance of having the right people in the right place at the right time and doing the right thing. It's a balancing act to keep an approachable image without letting a day to day nemesis manage you instead of the other way around. Here are four preliminary steps:

1. Have the right gate keeper in place. She will be able to tactfully and satisfactorily handle a lot of issues without them having to be referred to you. She will know when to refer to you and provide any necessary background information.
2. Think through all possible outcomes before making big decisions – put safeguards in place
3. Plan to touch base with your leading team members individually and regularly to limit the number of unplanned communications
4. Listen – plan rounds—sort of like the physician who makes rounds in the hospital – depending on the size of your organization it could be daily, weekly or monthly

Have a process for defining roles

As you can tell I am a strong proponent of spending the necessary time upfront rather than paying the consequences later on. So it is with being prepared for the unexpected and unwanted evil fiery dart. Make sure that your management team and the gatekeeper know when to make you aware of concerns or red flags. For instance, if there is an issue of consequence from a longtime supporter this should be reported to you immediately. Also if a negative trend has been identified, this too should be brought to your attention. Any personnel issue that has the potential to rise to a high level must be known about. Any threat to the reputation of your organization is of the utmost importance to you—the leader. These are just a few of the types of issues that can arise.

If an issue has been handled by your gatekeeper or a member of the management team it's necessary for them to notify you and report on their resolution. Late surprises put you behind the eight ball. It is important for your staff to understand the importance of bringing you all details surrounding an issue before referring the problem to you. For instance, if a major donor does not believe he has been credited for the high level of his giving you will need to see actual numbers from accounting. It is also imperative that you have all background information from the donor's perspective. Train your management team in advance to bring the issue to you along with needed detail and where appropriate a recommended solution. If there is a potential personnel problem you'll need to see past history and all internal and external information that may apply. You'll also need any regulatory government and organization policy information that may pertain.

The problem with distractions if not processed correctly they can cause excessive tension throughout your day. If your mindset switches to the distraction you will tire more quickly and are more likely to lose mental focus for your daily objectives. When the crisis call comes – and it will – if you're not pre-programmed with a process to handle it, frustration and worry can zap your strength. Otherwise be as prepared and organized as possible to handle everything. A cluttered desk filing system can hinder your ability to find things in the midst of a crisis.

Skill and knowledge that will help bring about resolve to crisis more quickly includes the following: decisiveness, knowing when to delegate, ability to say no, controls and policies in place, responsibility and authority clearly defined and finally—well established principles.

When your daily script has an unexpected scene

The unexpected will come your way for sure. It's actually part of what makes the leadership job exciting. No matter how clearly you lay out your pathway you can expect some pebbles and boulders along the way. Head your big problems off at the pass and train your management team to do the same. Don't let things fester until they become something bigger than you could have imagined. However, also don't sweat the small stuff. Understanding the difference between a small thing that has the potential to become a big thing and a small thing that will forever remain so can be a time and sanity saver! This is part of that "it" factor that we talked about earlier. Experience helps but some people are just better at recognizing and weeding out the small stuff that's going nowhere.

My older cousin Leona and her husband Tom had six girls. We had two children – a boy and a girl. I asked her one time how she managed. She said, "We don't sweat the small stuff." I have thought about that a lot over the years. She was quite a bit older than me and several of her children were grown by the time mine came along. So, when the small stuff happened and it did I was determined not to sweat it. That piece of advice has merit in all areas of life and definitely in the workplace.

When an unexpected crisis call comes, own up to your mistakes. If your organization has made an error admit to it and be prepared to tell what you're going to do to make sure that it doesn't happen again. Also, whatever you can do to rectify it in the current time frame – just do it. Perception can play a role here as well. You may know you have done no wrong but if there is a perception by the other person that you have – remember that perception is truth to the beholder. If you are the chief leader, don't take credit for a wrong not committed but always strive to take the high road and be the bigger person. Discuss things in such a way that the person sees that you understand and have heard their side of it. You would be surprised at how often people don't necessarily want you to "fix it" rather they just want to be heard. This is a great time for those active listening skills.

Now what about those daily interruptions that just seem to keep on coming? I had two members of my management team that handled their communications with me entirely different. One had a super system. She met with me weekly and brought a plain manila folder with her. In it she had a list of things that she wanted to talk to me about. She also would have little sticky notes and other pieces of important information included such as letters or notes that she had received and wanted me to know about. We would go down the list one by one and at the end everything had an agreed upon action. The issues were correctly identified as things I should know and have say about and our meetings did not generally take more than twenty minutes or so.

The other management team member emailed and called me numerous times every week day and sometimes on weekends to ask for guidance or advice on the "small stuff" she shouldn't be sweating – let along be bringing to me. The issues ranged from the mundane to the insane. Needless to say even through coaching the problem was not rectified. When emotional intelligence is missing it can become your weakest link to success.

It's important to have a planned time to make phone calls, answer emails, oversee administrative issues, think and review progress. Take time each day to spend time with your administrative assistant as gate keeper she is the "hub" of your organization. Having the right person in this position is extremely important. He or she can determine the urgency level of an issue and will know whether an interruption is called for or whether it can wait for a scheduled meeting time. Make sure she has a list of people you want to talk to at any time.

Keep your calendar fluid enough to make room for an unexpected urgency. In order to conduct a quick analysis keep an informal log for about a week. Make note of your scheduled and unscheduled actions including phone calls, meetings, email responses and all relevant actions and interactions. Then take time to analyze how well you're doing in the choices of how you spend your time. Have your staff conduct this exercise about once every two years or so. In the non-profit world there is always something important demanding your time. It's up to you to identify the most important and prioritize from there. Think about it, there is always one more expense you can delete from your budget if given the effort. The same goes for how you spend your time. You can always delete one not so necessary action to make room for something more important. However, don't delete your time for strategic thinking for the future. After all, without a successful future you will be left with only the past.

Balancing your time effectively may be the most important thing you have to do. It's quite a balancing act to guard your time wisely without seeming like you have a closed door policy. I was interviewing a person for a management level position one time and was taken aback by one of his answers. He said, "I have an open door policy and have gone so far as to take the door off of my office to make the point." He went on to say that there were other rooms that he could use for private conversations. Now, that is an interruption waiting to happen – all the time. As chief executive I had my door open during certain times of the day and closed at others. The closed door was a sign that I could not be disturbed during that time however, being as consistent as possible assured everyone that I was accessible during a reasonable amount of time.

Don't let stardom and ego get in the way

So far I've addressed the unexpected interruption from the perspective of one who would like to eliminate them as much as possible. Let's make sure you, the leader, do not let your ego get in the way. Having someone ask for your advice or help to solve their problems can make one feel important. Also there are some who just desire to stay informed and to know all the latest gossip. This is of course meaning beyond the need for no major surprises. So, take an honest evaluation of your own motives. Self-awareness is critical for a great leader. If you're one who avoids confrontation at all cost you may fear offending others by not making time for them immediately. No is an important word but it's also important to know when and how to use it effectively and tactfully.

Don't encourage your staff to bring all of their problems to you, rather encourage independent problem solving, innovative initiative, calculated risk-taking and decision-making. However, do be there to answer important questions and provide support along the way while providing the tools they need to succeed.

Adlib only when necessary

Being accessible does not have to mean being made vulnerable to ongoing unexpected interruptions at any and all times of your workday. By giving your staff members individually scheduled attention will eliminate the need for excessive interruptions. Flexibility is a necessity but having a process in place will still mean that you are in charge of the unexpected rather than the unexpected being in charge of you when you come to the end of the scenario.

Chapter Five

It's all about Relationships

"Our fingerprints don't fade from the lives we've touched"
—Remember Me

It takes a cast

What is it that you're trying to accomplish? You will need the support, cooperation, commitment, conviction and passion of others to win the Oscar or in business terms to exceed your goals! It takes a special ability to build great relationships with staff, board, donors, volunteers and the community. It's interesting that if you look at your greatest strength and then gaze straight across the spectrum your greatest weakness will usually be staring back at you. So as you look at your capability for building good relationships also make sure you're not using your strength to a fault. Know when to hold 'um and know when to fold "um.

Everyone can't be the leading sales person so make sure that your team members with the best relational skills are on the front line. Active listening is first on the list for building a solid relational foundation. More often than we would like to admit we're thinking about our reply rather than hearing every word. Granted sometimes the subject matter is not too exciting and boredom can easily set in but to the other person it's his most important thought for the moment.

It's critical to develop good listening skills. Face it in order to have good communication going forward you have to have the important information from your last visit. There are listening strategies you can use to cue the other person that you are hearing what's being said. Your cue can be something as simple as nodding your head in agreement or simply saying "I understand". If you need additional facts, merely ask, "Can you please clarify that a little more?" Feelings often enter in; therefore, reflect back to show that you understand saying something like, "evidently you feel like you were not treated fairly", or "that must have been a difficult experience for you." In order to make sure you're both on the same page reflect back what you have heard. "I understand then that you are going forward with what you originally planned." Some sort of summary feedback is helpful as well. "Nature has given to men one tongue, but two ears that we may hear from others twice as much as we speak" Epictetus

Don't get ahead of the plot

Don't go in to any important discussion with preconceived ideas this breaks down communication at the onset. However, do go in with all the facts you have to date and be prepared to substantiate your rationale and then courteously let him do the same. Always agree with as much as you can with the other person and give credit where credit is due. Never make your differences personal.

Fundraising is often more accurately called "friend-raising". Fundraising is not the activity of getting money out of people for your cause. It is rather an opportunity for a person to become a part of something bigger than self and to have significant impact upon one of the world's problems.

Regardless of what many people think, begging to a prospective donor is not good practice. Desperation does not reflect confidence. Just as in all walks of life, perspective donors want to go with a winner. They want to partner with success and become a part of making something significant happen. Do your homework before the first donor meeting. Make sure you know everything possible about her record of giving, family history, personal and civic interests and political interest if applicable. This information will help form a focus for your visit and create a level for your ask when the time is right. Your first visit is not the right time unless there are special circumstances. But it is a time to begin building a relationship. Ask questions and show interest in their answers. It's helpful to ask advice related to her area of expertise.

A door opener is your very best point of entry. This is someone with whom you already have a good relationship and one who is an influencer but also has access to your prospective donor. Sometimes this person phones ahead to provide a soft introduction but of course the best scenario is if he accompanies you on the visit.

I like to apply the 50% rule. I recommend spending 50% of your time listening and learning and the other 50% telling the story of your cause and why it's important. Be sure and integrate information about the strengths of your organization and why you're the ones to accomplish this feat. Mention other influential persons involved with the cause. Using a broad brush, explain your vision and speak of a strong foundation upon which to build. Always present your need in the positive perspective. The woe is "us" story is not your best bet. Don't end the meeting without setting the stage for a next move. Friend-raising is all about moves or actions which lead to your final goal. Statistics can be helpful but use them in moderation focusing instead on telling a poignant story.

The co-start strategy

In our world centered on technology, it's not necessarily the norm to build a program around one-on-one visits but they are still important. Technology has its place in fundraising and I encourage using webs, email, Facebook, twitter and the like. However, this should not be to the loss of face to face relationships. There's something about sitting with a person and looking straight into their eyes and their heart. This is how lasting relationships are created.

When you analyze your bottom line from the previous year set your goal for increase. Let's say it calls for an increase of 10%. If you made twenty face to face visits last year, consider increasing that number to thirty or forty in the New Year.

Your first visit is just a small part of building a base for friendship. Follow-up is extremely important. There's a myriad of ways you can do this. Begin with a thank you that highlights some of the issues from your first visit. It's a good idea to include some information that takes them to a next step of knowledge or action. Birthday and holiday cards are old standards that still work well. Email has its place but don't overlook the use of snail mail so that you can add a handwritten note.

If you see an article in the paper regarding your new found friend, cut it out and send it along with a congratulatory note. She may be chairing an event or there may be good news about her spouse or children. Our family went to the same chiropractor for years. If anyone of us were mentioned in the paper regarding a sports win – or in my case effort in my hospital or nonprofit work we would get a copy of the article in the mail with an attached hand written note. This was a terrific connector and reminded us of how much we enjoyed our friendship with this health professional. It sent the message that he cared about our lives outside of his office.

The ability to read between the lines

Let's look at the service industry. How does the relational behavior of your wait staff influence your thought about tipping? A great waiter has the ability to "read" his guests and temper his communication accordingly. The trick is to quickly build a rapport without becoming intrusive. Some people are very outgoing and expressive often going so far as to invite the wait staff to sit down for a short visit. Wait-staff that can gauge the right level of communication will garner an exceptional tip. We went to Destin Florida to celebrate our anniversary. My husband is one of those very expressive individuals. We visited a restaurant on the water and were served by a young man who caught on to our personalities very quickly. I was impressed with how he understood my husband's need to build a friendly rapport while listening carefully to some special dietary requirements that I expressed. He handled it all perfectly and not only did he get a good tip but rather than go to another restaurant like we had planned we returned there the next evening. Steve, our waiter, left us wanting to try other things on the menu and enjoy his friendly and detailed service once again.

By the time we left Destin, we had frequented the restaurant three times and felt like we were telling a friend good-bye. We did go to the restaurant one last time but Steve was not there and it was an entirely different experience. Our food service was correct and timely but there was never a relationship developed. It was not an experience that would have brought us back for more. We will not forget Steve and will make it a point to go back there when we are in the area.

Randy is the manager of the auto service department that we use. He has taken the time to get to know us and gives the sense that he will handle my car as if it is his own. He has shown me that he is trustworthy and makes the effort to know the last time we were in and for what. If it doesn't need fixing he doesn't fix it. He has bent over backwards to meet our scheduling needs. Sometimes my husband just stops in to say hi if he's in the neighborhood. I recently bought a new car at the dealer where he is service manager. Randy talked to our sales person and told him what good clients we were and directed him to treat us right. I had done my homework and knew what constituted a good deal. We got not just a good deal but rather a great deal mostly attributed to Randy's assistance. It's all about the relationship he has built with us over time.

We all have had a teacher or mentor that we can never forget. It's not just about the grade at the end of the year but just as important—the experience of the journey. Going back through history it's easy to identify elected officials – even at the highest level who won the vote due to their ability to build rapport sometimes regardless of knowledge or experience levels.

There's always something of interest to be learned from others. The thing is the other person can tell if you're really interested in what they have to say. It's such a basic principle to make yourself aware of the other persons' interests and needs and yet it seems like we sometimes have to be reminded to put others first when practicing the art of friendship building.

Connecting with people isn't difficult but it takes time and effort. Successful leaders do the initiating. They make the first move, the first connection with sincerity and honesty. When you reach out first there are many examples that confirm that the other person will reach back to you.

Making the most of a red carpet event

Sometimes your only opportunity to speak one-on-one with your targeted individual is at some sort of special event or reception. Think about who is going to be there before you arrive. Always hold out your hand and speak your name first and clearly so that they aren't forced to remember or guess who you are. Make the connection but don't talk business unless the circumstance warrants. Create a friendly rapport but don't monopolize his time. If it goes well, get his business card and follow-up.

Whenever I sent a member of the management team to a conference or in particular to a national leadership meeting of our parent organization, I sent them with objectives. They were given a connect list which usually included high level leaders of the organization. Sometimes the objective of the connection was just getting face and name time as a representative from our chapter. Every connection needs objectives even if they are short and simple. No meeting should be held without purpose. How will you know if you have succeeded if you have no purpose?

Onscreen likability key to building relationships

Interpersonal skills are important in making those lasting relationships and providing a pathway easy to follow. There are recognizable qualities in a person with exceptional interpersonal skills.

- Understands the behaviors of people in general
- Presents an approachable and positive persona
- Excels at gaining buy-in
- Easily accepted by others even in sticky situations
- Builds a trusting rapport
- Knows how to get along with co-workers
- Is often the peacemaker
- Attracts favorable attention
- Has influence
- Displays sincerity when dealing with others
- Has the ability to relate easily
- Respects the opinions of others
- Displays appropriate assertiveness without becoming abrasive
- Represents the organization well
- Easily develops and maintains communication with others
- Has the ability to put others at ease

- Has a friendliness and warmth that is evident
- Is interested in what others have to say
- Knows how to guide a conversation without dominating it

Exercise your authority with wisdom and caution. A dictator with an iron rod may get people to do things but great leadership does not operate in that way. Wisdom is all wrapped up in your values. Your values will lead you as you lead others.

Chapter Six

Reviews are for Reading

"I'll be back" —**Terminator**

Return for Review

Know where you are at all times. Know why and how you got there so that you can make wise decisions going forward. You may have a top notch CPA and that is as it should be. She will be able to provide accurate numbers. As Chief Executive of your organization it's up to you to look back over the numbers and analyze what they mean. Ask for all the data you need to get a clear picture of your status.

For instance, be sure and conduct a comparison study using bottom line numbers and percentages of past performances. Look at trends nationally and know where you are in comparison. One of my former organizations had a great vice President of Finance and he could provide excellent oversight for the compilation of numbers. He also could spot red financial flags and create a great base for budget development. However, we amazed even ourselves by how well our combined perspective of the numbers worked toward our success.

Since I am not an accountant or CPA he provided data in whatever form that I asked. You would think that accounting would always fall in a category and the results would be black and white. The bottom line does not change but there are definite considerations to be made. Some need the expertise of the CPA and some need a piercing eye of the Chief Executive.

Some nonprofit organizations have multiple grants covering the same type of work or involving the operations of the same staff members. It's true that the bean counter will have a guide to go by and most likely get the money allocated correctly. However, silos within the organization can sometimes stifle information flow. However, you as the person in charge need to have a review and understand what allocated decisions were made and why. With the increased oversight by the federal government it is even more imperative that you know and understand your accounting process. It is imperative that you spell out how the money will be spent and then spend it in that way making sure it is accounted for in the same way.

The buck stops with you. Know what you need to know and stay on top of the details. It's not unusual to get a recommendation or two in the letter from your auditor. They are interested in making your organization as risk free as possible. However, it is important to follow-up on their recommendations and do make changes as recommended. Since our organization started out small and grew into a large organization over time, the recommendations grew as well. Each year as we grew we added additional barriers to risk. We did reach a point when there were no more recommendations in our letter from the auditor because we continued to decrease our risk as we added employees to provide more separations in financial duties.

Even though your CPA and auditors are very engaged in the review process it's important for you to understand the process and at some time meet with the auditor yourself. Make sure that your accounting department is as prepared as possible before the auditor arrives. The unaudited financials should be fairly close to the auditors' findings. Because of regulations of the federal government the auditor is limited as to what kind of assistance she can provide in your accounting process.

Review your compensation guidelines regularly. Know how your management team's package compares to that of the chief executive. It's the kind of information that's scrutinized more carefully now. They also look at perks and extra benefits such as bonuses. Safe Harbor is a term used by the IRS. Make sure you have taken steps to ensure reasonableness of executive compensation. Obtain comparability data from credible sources and seek external expertise.

For nonprofits with revenues of $1 million or more the 990 reporting requirements changed drastically in 2008. A 990-EZ or short form was required for organizations with revenues of $25,000 or more. In 2009, the threshold for filing the new 990 long form dropped to $500,000 in nonprofit gross revenue. In 2010 the amount dropped to $200,000. Clearly the IRS is not taking the new filing requirements lightly. It has already revoked the tax-exempt status of many nonprofits for non-compliance. When such organizations lose their tax-exempt status they have to go through the process and expense of re-applying. The IRS rationale for imposing these strict new requirements on nonprofits is simple: Past abuses, such as inflated salaries and unsound conflicts of interest have raised public concern. Transparency to the public is the goal. The new 990 form is very detailed and requires new policies and procedures to be in place. Make sure that you chose an accounting firm with extensive nonprofit experience. Familiarize yourself with the 990 form and ensure that your organization actually meets the requirements. Each board member should receive a copy of your 990 report as well as it being made available to the public.

Ensure that your employee handbook is reviewed regularly and in sync with appropriate HR practices and in line with government regulations. This is a responsibility delegated to ones with HR expertise. However, you need to be aware of any recommended changes and familiar with the basics of the manual. There is always a possibility of an issue that comes along and challenges how something is written in the handbook.

It actually can be risky to become too wordy under some categories in your handbook. However, it must be clearly written and easily understood. So the bottom line is to make sure you have knowledgeable staff or advisors to oversee the completing and updating of your employee handbook and to also be aware of what's in it. Not all nonprofits have an HR specialist on staff. This does not lessen the need for that kind of expertise. Seek a specialist to serve on your board of directors or to serve in an advisory capacity as a volunteer.

Finance and human resources are two departments with a higher liability risk. Therefore, you cannot afford to leave the entire oversight to others. Remember the buck stops with you even though the board of directors is legally liable. Your question to answer is this: "What is the outside chance that something could happen and what can we do to head it off at the pass?" It's your role to foresee possible consequences of numbers, actions, policies and plans and make changes accordingly.

Don't misunderstand this warning. I don't recommend that you get tied down in day to day minutia. However, it is important to know what you need to know and delegate everything that makes sense to those "right" people you have in place.

A scene you may be familiar with

How about the attending physician for a hospitalized patient? The doctor is not there overseeing the patient 24-7 but he has competent nurses and others to take care of the frontline work. He guides the patient to health by prescribing appropriate directions and then reviewing the nurses' reports. Then she assesses the patient in person periodically. There are evaluating tests given along the way for her to examine what's going on internally.

That is why it's so important for you to review the diagnostic evaluation reviews provided by your staff regularly so that you can determine what's really going on. Evaluation can mean several things in the nonprofit. It can refer to the monthly financial reports or feedback from the community in general on how you're doing as an organization. So, the evaluation can be come in written form and could even be a focus group. What's measured can be managed.

Show me the money – but also excellence in programming!

When conducting an educational forum it's helpful to find out what the participants know coming in and at the conclusion of the program. This can serve as a guide to the effectiveness of your program. Also, it's important to track the number of participants and their demographics. All information will be helpful to improve your service program. Dig a little deeper to find out what else they would like you to provide a long with their reasoning of how and why. Find ways to measure impact and outcomes at every turn as later you can combine this information with current trends, technology improvements and the knowledge of what's left to be done.

As chief executive you need to know the organization internally and externally and provide guidance and leadership overall. Ensure that there is an effective information communication flow to and through you. Maintain fiscal control and strategically oversee all aspects of the association. Remember in order to go forward to a successful finish you have to go back and review all necessary data and feedback.

Chapter Seven

There is more to believe in than Santa Claus Virginia

"Just because you can't see something doesn't mean it isn't there"
—Stepmom

Non-fiction = believe it

Many people like to call it mind over matter. I like to call it belief over unbelief. Believe those things that create success as though they are possible. Do not believe in failure. You are the gatekeeper of your thoughts and for that matter – emotions. Emotions are a necessary and important part of life. In fact I can't imagine how void life would be without them. However, your emotions can lie to you – so can your thoughts. There's actually a well-known proverb that relays the message that whatever we think we are – we are.

Keeping it "reel"

I cannot count the times they re-ran the video of the 2011 NASCAR championship race. It came down to a two man race between Tony Stuart and Carl Edwards and was truly won by belief and "will". Tony did not do well in the first part of the racing season and even he spoke about his doubts to "get there" this year. However, somewhere along the way to the last ten races his mindset changed. He began to visualize himself as champion. The CHASE actually consists of the last ten races for the year. Tony started winning but was still lagging behind in points from Carl Edwards who had led in points for weeks. It came down to the last race and Carl was favored to win the championship. However, Tony was focused and believed that it was his to win. Oddly enough the only way he could win the championship was to win the race. This was not the case for Carl if Tony did not win Carl was ensured the championship even if he didn't win. They were in first and second place throughout the end of the race but Tony did win. This meant they tied in points for the year but that Tony won the championship. Even the sports announcers gave credit to his mindset change. It will go down in history if not the most – one of the most memorable championship races of all time.

Some experts estimate that success is 80% attitude and 20 percent aptitude. Martin Seligman, Ph.D. a professor of psychology at the University of Pennsylvania set out to conclude the importance of thinking positive. He examined positive mental attitude in reference to job performance related to employees of a major life insurance company.

What he found was remarkable. Those who anticipated a "yes" response outsold their negative co-workers by 37%. These results did not necessarily match their knowledge on the standard industry test. Believing gives you an edge!

By presenting the image of confidence, self-assurance and happiness you give others the impression that you have things well in and are headed toward success. Others will then in turn be more eager to follow your lead or direction. It's easy to think like a winner when all is going well. The key to great leadership is to maintain "belief" when challenges come your way.

Don't let the critics shake your belief

The battle for success is in your mind. It's the battle of whether to believe or not believe that it can be done and that you are the one to lead. Whatever thoughts have your attention will guide your pathway and just knowing something is not quite the same as believing it with unshakable purpose. Too many people believe they have no control over what thoughts flow through their mind but that is not the case. If doubt is given enough attention it can begin to monopolize your actions as well. As the leader of your team, you set the tone, the belief and motivational pathway to success. There will always be critics who say it can't be done just because they have never seen it before.

Have you ever noticed that even a good ball team can go astray once their leader starts to lose focus and belief? That's when we see an unexpected upset and the other team becomes the champion. Leading has a measure of "cheerleading" involved. There's something about having confidence in the team leader and believing that she knows what she is doing and that she is leading the team to success. Cheerleading along the way helps keep the team energized and feeling good about their efforts.

A great leader can see qualities in others that they might not even be able to recognize in themselves. I had a boss like that early in my career. He had belief in my ability to learn new things quickly and to take on broader responsibilities. I started out as a part time entry level employee and in five years was serving on the management team overseeing three department areas. His ability to see this potential in me and to provide an environment to learn and grow evolved into success for me and for the organization. My trust in his proven success was the catalyst that developed faith in myself to grow beyond what I had earlier imagined. As leaders we have the awesome responsibility to recognize potential and this goes back to finding the "right" person in the first place. The "right" person may not need to be fully developed depending on the position. However, your ability to recognize potential comes by paying attention, listening between the lines and carving out a pathway for learning and broadening responsibilities for that "right" person.

It's been proven over and over again that children who grow up with parents who believe in them have a much easier road to success. The same goes for a workplace team with a leader who believes in their ability to succeed. There is not much more rewarding for a leader than to mentor a young employee with great potential and to watch them grow in stature and success. The key is to believe in the possibility of their success before you can actually see it. Or more aptly put to visualize it before you can actually see it come to pass. The beauty in this process is that somewhere along the way they begin to visualize it as well and their actions match their belief. You have to give your people with potential permission to take a risk. They need to know that you believe in them enough to manage the risk and to overcome any possible failure.

It's simple, what you think (or believe) you are capable of doing is what you are capable of doing. What you – the chief executive—thinks or believes his team is capable of doing will sooner or later be the label they will wear. A great leader has the ability to see farther than others see and to see more than others see and to see it before others see. This sets the stage for believing and leading others to believe as well.

Expanding the belief to a greater audience

Even the greatest marketing plan perfectly executed cannot bring about external success if the internal health of the organization is not founded on a sound-positive belief in the cause. Is your cause worth believing in? Can you easily build the case for why broad-based support is needed? Will corporations and foundations be able to see the impact of your proposed work? What will change if you are able to reach the goals of your cause? Do believe in the cause enough to keep at it when others are not yet convinced that your work is necessary or better yet a priority?

When a person believes strongly enough in a cause she will go to great lengths to see success. She will give herself options and alternatives when one door is closed. Believing brings about steadfastness and helps you weather the storm. It is not something to be based on loosely

Your Starring Role

gathered opinions but rather should be based on well researched data and real life experiences. You have got to be able to present a solid case to yourself and to others as to "why" the cause is so vitally important and "how" greatly your efforts if given the chance will have a powerful impact. Knowing you are on solid ground in your belief takes it out of just the emotional level and includes also the level of knowledge.

We have touched on the importance of believing in yourself with a confidence that you are the right person to lead the effort. It is such an important key to success it's worth taking a more detailed look. For sure there is a level of self-confidence that comes from good parenting when we are children. However, many have been able to overcome the effects of bad parenting and to approach life with self-confidence and success.

I was mentoring a young and somewhat inexperienced employee who had moved up to a supervisory level. She actually had the knowledge needed for that level but greatly lacked the self-awareness and confidence to lead. She explained that when she had to attend meetings with peers from the community she felt inadequate to represent our organization in the way that she should. She said she felt inferior and ill equipped.

We worked on this from several aspects. First we developed a self-talk message for her to actually speak out loud. There's something about hearing words spoken that seems to have more impact. Next I recommended that she do research on everyone scheduled to attend the next community leader meeting. I told her to use Facebook, Google and the local newspaper. She was to find out everything she could about each person and develop some talk points so that she would be prepared no matter which attendee she came in contact with.

Thirdly she was directed to study the agenda for the meeting and look for ways to enter in to the discussion in representation of our organization. It was recommended that she develop talking points and practice them in front of a mirror. The follow-up report from the meeting was good. She felt more comfortable in the setting and was able to speak more freely and with confidence. Competence doesn't compensate for insecurity. Insecure leaders are not capable of leading self to success let alone leading others. Insecure persons tend to "take" more than they "give" and this characteristic does not generate confidence in subordinates. They often place barriers and limitations on their staff and the organization for that matter due to insecurity based in fear.

Believing in oneself does not mean that you have to have certainty about everything. It does mean that you have to have clarity in what you are directed to do. Clarity breeds confidence in yourself and your followers. Along the way your trust muscle can be tested. There is always a possibility that someone will let you down. Humans have that capability. But if you lose your trust muscle – you begin to lose confidence and the freedom to give others reign. It all goes back to having the right people in place so that you do not experience this often if at all.

Leaders who believe in the cause and self are viewed as single-minded. They have nothing to hide and therefore, no need to pretend or fear. Integrity is part of their character. Believing in one's self allows for predetermining what you will be regardless of what circumstances you may face. This type of leader brings about strength to the team. How often have we heard it said that someone is self-motivated or a self-starter? Guess what? This takes belief in oneself to move forward without hand holding. Motivation is a characteristic of passion.

- "Nobody can make you feel inferior without your consent" **Eleanor Roosevelt**
- "A successful person is one who can lay a firm foundation with the bricks that others throw at him or her" **David Brinkley**
- "Whether you think you can or can't you are right" **Henry Ford**
- "If you hear a voice within you say you cannot paint, then by all means paint" **Vincent Van Gogh**

- "I am not a has-been. I am a will be" **Lauren Bacall**
- "You have to expect things of yourself before you do them" **Michael Jordon**
- "Aerodynamically the bumblebee shouldn't be able to fly but the bumblebee doesn't know that – it goes flying anyway" **Mary Kay Ash**
- "Without a humble but reasonable confidence in your own power you cannot be successful or happy" **Norman Vincent Peale**
- "There are many qualities that make a great leader but having strong beliefs, being able to stick with them through popular and unpopular times is the most important characteristic" **Rudy Giuliani**

Dorothy Neddermeyer, PhD warns that the concept of championing oneself is becoming foreign to one's view of oneself within the world. She sees evidence that it has become shameful to believe in yourself publicly. She gives the partial definition of championing as a supporter or defender of a person or cause. Drdorothy.netArticleSource.http://Ezine,Articles.com/?expert=Dorothy_M_Neddermyer_phD

Belief in oneself does not come without preparedness. However, preparing to a point where you become too paralyzed to move without more preparation is counter-productive. Then you are into the paralysis of analysis. For me personally, I did not come to a point of believing in myself without knowing that there is a great God that provides dreams, inspiration and guidance and is the ultimate leader of myself and my team.

Action!

Begin! Just start at point A and you're on your way. Sometimes the first step is the most difficult. But at this point you have a vision and the plan is spelled out. You know who is to do what and they are equipped and prepared.

Manage your expectations knowing that you will come up against the unexpected along the way. It's similar to when you take a trip and move along quite nicely either by directions from your map or GPS system. Then it happens, you come to a detour sign. So it will be with your action plan. You as the leader are the GPS system placed to navigate your team over, under or around the detour until you're back on course. This is not a time to lose courage and it is definitely not a time for your team to see your fear. Notice I did not say that you might not have fear but it is not the time to let it lead you. Otherwise, manage your fear and manage the detour. It's necessary to manage your expectations throughout. Don't set them too low or base them on delusions of grandeur. However, take the team to a place never before traveled as you lead the team to new heights. Make a decision based upon your research, experience and the desired result if a course change is needed. Changing course does not produce failure but stopping or retreating can.

However, it can and does happen too frequently that because of challenges or the assumption that someone else will do it, leaders sit on their belief without acting. The truth is, you are that someone else! You are the one to act and you are the one to lead.

Chapter Eight

The Ending Belongs to you and your Team

"Life is like a movie—write your own ending."
—Jim Hensen (America's puppeteer)

Final credits are yours

Orson Wells once said, "If you want a happy ending that depends, of course on where you stop your story." How true. We're all familiar with the saying, "never say die" and so it is with great leadership. We all remember the sad but true story of the Titanic that was later made into a great classic movie. During the time of this writing a cruise liner had a recent major tragedy off the shores of Italy. There are several dead and some still missing. All of this happened because of extremely poor judgment and leadership by the Captain. First of all he caused the ship to crash upon a cliff like area in the ocean by purposely veering off course.

Your Starring Role

This radical move caused the ship to hang up on huge rocks causing it to turn on its' side and take on water. As unbelievable as it may seem, it has been reported that he did this merely to honk at bystanders on shore. It has been reported that he only made things worse by abandoning ship; even after his superior yelled orders to go back on board and organize the rescue effort. Every leadership quality you would expect from a Captain was missing. The ending he wrote was not one anyone in a position of leadership would want. But, he wrote the ending and he owns it. Other than there being a tragedy on board a large ship, there were no other similarities between these two Captains.

You own your ending as well. What will you do with your short term wins and your losses along the way? A loss is not a loss unless that's where you stop. A loss can be your stepping stone to success. If something doesn't work out the way you planned you now have information you did not have before – it will not work as originally planned. However, don't live there. Spend more time examining what worked and tweak it to work even better. After the setback it may be time to change course a bit but not haphazardly like the Captain spoke of in Italy. Changing course should only be done by calculating the risk and planning a better way.

Your Starring Role

Your team members are stakeholders in the ending you write for them. As cast and crew, they make it happen but as Captain you chart their course along the way. Using our shipwrecked Captain again as an example; just think about how many lives he affected by using poor judgment by an impulsive self-serving action that ultimately lost life, the ship and his own prospect for life quality going forward.

Now I am pretty sure that none of your decisions would quite have this impact. However, you will be charting the course. Many are depending on you for direction, guidance and oversight. They will expect you to steer them back into smooth waters when the going gets rough.

A great ending will turn your vision into reality. To reach that point start out right, keep it going in the middle and end strong! End, n 1. Extreme or concluding part 2. Close 3. Purpose 4. Result. It's interesting that if you add three letters to "end" you get "endless". Once your vision has come to fruition your possibilities are endless going forward. Now you have only just begun and especially if you are celebrating a successful ending. You already know how to dream and what comes next. Having a good team in place, the sky's the limit as they say.

Produce a great ending

- Break up the word impossible to I M possible
- Feel like there is no other alternative than the ending you have chosen
- Develop one that is made up of a series of great choices and start at the beginning
- Never end leaving things just as you found them (great leaders take things to a better place)
- See the end you desire before you begin
- Consider what pitfalls may come your way and plan accordingly
- Bring together the best minds on your team and brainstorm for improvements
- Be willing to revise your ending as long as it's for the better and does not contradict the vision
- When your team has completed the project and done all they can do ... do the one more exceptional thing that will put your team efforts way over the top!

Your vision is a living thing. As you reach what you think to be the conclusion you will see that what lives has the potential to go on living as long as it's still growing.

The End
(Is awaiting your leadership)

www.ingramcontent.com/pod-product-compliance
Ingram Content Group UK Ltd.
Pitfield, Milton Keynes, MK11 3LW, UK
UKHW041944230426
12048UKWH00008B/128